Farming For Beginners

The Backyard Animal Farm Guide To Farming Sheep, Raising Chickens, Turkeys, Pigs, Milking Cows, Goats, Honey Bees, Cattle Farming, and More!

By

Frank Begley

Table of Contents

Introduction

It wasn't that long ago that living on a farm was the norm. People produced their food and traded excess product with neighbors so that everyone had the 'groceries' they needed. Children in those days knew where and how their food was produced and participated in running the farm. The grocery stores we shop in today didn't even exist until the mid-1940's and yet now that is where the vast majority of us get our food.

Although it is convenient to shop at one location and buy products that taste good and satisfy our hunger, the consequences of eating this way is all too obvious. Our grandparents and great grandparents were much healthier than our generation. They were tougher too. At 10 years old, many of our great grandparents were likely up at dawn and doing chores around the farm. The children of today have eyes fixed to screens and bodies atrophied by lack of movement.

By farming, you can go back in time and embrace the nutritional density of the food you produce as well as the lifestyle that enables you to produce. Instead of willfully ignoring or rallying against the plight of animals raised on factory farms, you can choose an ethical way to nourish your body. This clip from a Joel Salatin interview should inspire.

Whether you are a 'prepper' or simply like to be prepared for extreme weather events, farming is ideal. When there are runs on grocery stores and empty shelves, you can be confident that food production will continue, and your family will be able to eat.

When those extreme events are in play, there will probably be an excess of food that you can potentially sell. Farmer's markets are becoming increasingly common, and if your farm is fairly close to a major urban center, you may want to explore that option. In most places, regulations are few surrounding selling garden produce and eggs. Selling meat and dairy is an entirely different matter.

If you are planning on selling meat and dairy, you need to look very carefully at the regulations surrounding this in your area. For instance, selling raw milk is OK in some jurisdictions but completely illegal in others. The laws surrounding meat are especially onerous. You may be required to have your animals processed in a slaughter facility in order to sell your meat to the public. It can be difficult to find a slaughterhouse that processes the type of animal you are raising, and it is likely that practices followed are less than humane.

So get to know your laws before you even purchase your first animal as you might find that following the law is more burdensome that you can cope with. If you have the means, you may want to consider setting up a butchery on your farm. If done properly, you can usually find a way to follow your local laws while farming the way you want. Joel Salatin has done just that. There are many entertaining books written by him discussing the subject of building an ethical farm business.

Bookworm Fertilizer

Work intelligently. Some of your neighbors will be innovative, but most will be doing things exactly like their parents farmed. There are people all over North America that are embracing old farming methods and splicing in more efficient ways using new technology.

Embrace old ideas and try and learn as much as possible about how animals were raised before factory farming became the norm. Walk through your pasture and find out what is growing on your land; the grass species and the soil. Be aware of your plot of earth from below the ground up. Consider using permaculture principles to help shape your farm.

Choosing Land

Forage

Where you choose to farm affects what you farm greatly. Forage quality, drainage (or lack thereof), trees, and what your neighbors are growing can help or harm your venture.

Forage is plant material that your grazing animals will be consuming. These will include forbs, legumes, and grasses. You can find information on different types of forage here:

When it comes to foraging, the more variety, the better. Different species of plants mature at different times. Their protein and sugar content vary depending on the type, the maturity of the species and even the time of day. Having a variety of species on your land ensures that there is ample nutrition available for your animals throughout the growing season. If there is not a variety of forage available, this can be remedied by obtaining a variety of seeds. In areas that experience frost, 'frost seeding' in early spring is the most cost effective option.

For areas that don't experience frost or for seeding done later in the spring or summer, straightforward broadcast seeding is your best option. Broadcast seeding should be done on bare patches and preferably after the area has been intensively grazed.

Water

Too much or too little water can be a difficult problem to overcome. In an ideal world, you will be farming on land that you own the water rights to. However depending on where you buy, this may prove difficult. It goes without saying that it is extremely important that your animals have access to fresh water at all times. As long as there is water available somewhere on your land, a pump can transfer it to exactly where it's needed.

It is a good idea to speak to your neighbors and find out if there have been any issues of regular flooding in the area. Wet, soggy ground does not make for happy animals. It's totally fine if there are a few marshy areas, but there should be ample, well-drained land for your stock to lie down.

Mud is the bane of every farmer's existence and makes doing all of your chores messy and difficult.

Community

If you're coming from an urban environment, you might think that it is perfectly natural to have no idea who your neighbors are. When you move to a farming community, your neighbors can be an enormous help.

Prior to purchasing a property it is essential that you find out who your neighbors are and what they do. If your closest neighbor uses lots of chemicals, it has the potential to impact the health of your pastures and your animals. Finding a property with like-minded neighbors can be extremely advantageous. By doing this, you can avoid potential conflicts, and there are sometimes opportunities to share work (such as processing chickens). Sharing seldom used, expensive equipment can also be possible with neighbors who are thrift minded.

Also consider the broader community you are considering moving to. Wander around the nearby town and get a feel for the place. Speak to the man or woman who works at the post office. Have a cup of coffee at the local eatery and eavesdrop on those around you for a while. These are the people whose families will be socializing with yours and if you don't feel as though you will be able to 'fit in', perhaps you should consider settling elsewhere.

If you are planning on selling some of your farm products, it's a good idea to find out where the nearest farmers market is. If possible, plan to attend a market day and take a look at what is being offered for sale. If you're keen on selling honey and there are already four other people selling it in a relatively small community, it is best you find that out now rather than later.

Local laws can also affect what you are planning to farm. Depending on your State or Province, local laws may prevent you from either selling your product to the public or the way in which you may sell it. For instance, in many jurisdictions selling raw milk (unpasteurized) is illegal. In some cases, you can get around the law by altering your product so that it falls within the law. For example, you may be able to turn the raw milk into cheese and sell it without breaking any laws.

Once you have just about settled on where you want to buy, track down the local large animal vet. A vet that mostly neuters small dogs will likely not artificially inseminate cows. A good vet for a farmer will be willing to give you advice over the phone on how to treat your animal when appropriate. They will also be willing to drag themselves out of bed at 3am to help you pull a calf stuck in the birth canal.

Equipment & Tools

Every farm needs a pick-up truck. It doesn't need to be pretty; you just need to be able to throw stuff in the back of it and for it to start. Make sure it has enough horsepower to pull a small trailer and a tow hitch. It's probably best if it isn't in great shape because you'll be less likely to care when it gets caked in mud inside and out. You will also need to purchase an all-terrain vehicle (ATV). If you have small children, you may want to consider a safer design that is less likely to roll as ATV accidents are common.

If you will frequently be transporting animals, consider getting a small trailer. A small horse float will do the job fine. If you think you'll only need this piece of equipment once in a while, consider borrowing one from a neighbor or renting one. U-Haul rents horse floats in many areas.

Since your animals will need access to fresh water at all times, you will likely need to purchase a water pump, as well as some troughs. In the heat of summer, water left in above ground pipes can become very hot. Your animals will not want to drink hot water so try to have water flow continuously and use white PVC piping.

If your land does not currently have a perimeter fence, you will need to install one. You will need barbed wire and fence posts as well as a hydraulic post pounder. Find a post pounder to rent by the day as purchasing one is expensive and unless you're building fences for a living, not worth it. Consider hiring someone to help you build a fence that has experience. It is well worth the money to invest in doing the job well so that the infrastructure lasts, and your animals don't escape.

Animals You Won't be Eating

Predators

Depending on where you settle, your livestock will tempt certain local wild carnivores. Larger livestock will be a target for bears, mountain lions, wolves, and coyotes. Smaller livestock have these predators as well as smaller critters to worry watch out for. Raccoons, possums, snakes, foxes and weasels can leave chicken enclosures looking like a scene from a horror movie.

Wild predators are everywhere. They would like nothing more than to sneak onto your farm while you are sleeping and slaughter your animals. A secure place to roost in a portable coop can protect your chickens during the night, but larger livestock are very vulnerable to these poachers.

Losing livestock is difficult both financially speaking and emotionally. Even the most careful farmer loses some livestock to predators so try not to beat yourself up too much about it and instead focus your efforts on preventing further loss.

Many farmers use poisons to control pests – especially in the case of coyotes. It would be wise to avoid this widespread practice if you can help it. Condemning any animal to a painful death simply for acting on its natural instincts is inhumane and there are risks involved in introducing poison to any food chain. A better choice would be to use one of the natural deterrents mentioned below along with ensuring that your fences and pens are as secure as possible.

Man's Best or Most Irritating Friend

If you're moving from the city to the country with a 'city dog', beware. Hopefully, your dog is well-trained or at least skittish enough to stay close to the house. Otherwise, you may end up wishing you would have left rover with a relative. Dogs that have not been around livestock can wreak havoc. Larger dogs can decimate whole flocks of chickens. All dogs can cause larger animals endless amounts of stress when they are chased and barked at constantly. If you have one of these problems animals you will either need to train it to behave quickly or consider finding it another home.

Conversely, a well-trained working dog can be a farmer's best friend. If you have cattle or sheep, breeds such as border collies and kelpies can make excellent working companions. There are many other working breeds as well but be sure to only consider those who don't nip at livestock. Dogs that bite in order to have livestock obey them can cause stress in your animals.

A very popular breed used by ranchers around the world is Great Pyrenees dogs. These dogs are often raised with the livestock. Their loyalty should be to your livestock, not to you. If they want to be with you, they will sleep on your porch and be of little use for protecting your assets.

The Mouser

Every farm should have at least one cat. When you have livestock, you have feed. Where there is feed there will be mice and/or rats. These little rodents will eat your feed and are just not pleasant to have around. A good farm cat may not rid your farm of these rodents but they will at the very least control the population. Look for a kitten or full grown cat from a not so nearby farm (if it's an older cat, it might just decide it would rather live at 'home').

Do not raise a kitten that you want to be an outside cat in your house. Your house is off limits for this working cat. If it's cold, make sure it has a nice warm place to sleep in a shed or barn with lots of hay and maybe an old coat to lie on. If it's extremely cold, try to get a couple cats so they can keep warm together. Don't worry about getting a litter box for outdoor cats unless you want to clean a litter box. Fear not, Kitty will find a nice spot in your flower bed to do her business.

You may have mice in your house and if that's the case, get a house cat as well. Buy some cheap cat food that isn't so delicious that your cat doesn't have any desire to kill. Feed your cats generously but remember that a fat cat isn't going to catch anything.

One cat can easily turn into several cats. Even though neutering and spaying your cat does tend to diminish their mouse killing drive, it needs to be done. A generation or two ago, farmers controlled their cat population by drowning kittens. I'm guessing you didn't want to get back to nature in order to drown kittens so make an appointment with your local vet. Obviously the same goes for your farm dog. A bonus is that your animal will be way less likely to wander if they're not checking out the tomcat or bitch at the neighbors.

The Ass

It's improbable that you've ever fantasized about owning a donkey. There are few if any movies with a donkey as the hero. But a donkey can be a very good animal to have around, especially if you have wolves or coyotes in your vicinity. More about this unsung farm hero here:

Hay Burners

A long time ago, a horse was an essential animal to have on every farm. Now for most farmers they are not so affectionately referred to as 'hay burners'. This insulting phrase refers to how much food horses eat – their cost of upkeep. For most farmers, it makes far more sense to herd livestock by quad or foot depending on the size of your property.

Personality wise, horses often do not get along so well with other livestock. Being smarter than nearly all livestock except maybe goats and pigs; horses bully and can often injure other animals. If you spent your early years fantasizing about riding a horse through a field of wild flowers, by all means go for it. But it's a good idea to locate the closest glue factory just in case you change your mind (kidding!).

Planning Your Grazing

How Much Land or How Many Animals

How much land you're going to need in order to feed your animals is an extremely important calculation. If you underestimate, you could run out of pasture for your animals to graze and you'll end up having to sell your animals or end up with a hefty hay bill. Whether you're feeding cattle, goats or sheep; each animal is going to eat about 2.5-3% of its body weight each and every day. Exactly how much they eat will vary depending on how much energy is required to maintain their core body temperature. In colder climates, livestock can require up to 40% more food.

To calculate how much land you will need, figure out how many 'animal units' you plan to have. An 'animal unit' is based on 1,000 pounds of 'animal'. One animal unit can be one cow that weighs 1,000 pounds, 10 goats that are 100 pounds each or 200 chickens that are 5 pounds each. The next step is to take the number of animal units we are feeding and multiply that by 3% (what they'll eat per day). Using that calculation we know how much forage we'll need to provide the animals with on a daily basis.

Rotational Grazing

In order to maximize the productivity of your pasture (how much grass your land can grow), you need to implement some type of rotational grazing. Instead of treating your land as one big paddock, you separate it into several smaller paddocks. You then allow your livestock to graze one paddock at a time. By doing this you ensure that nearly all plants are being grazed, being fertilized (thanks to livestock dung and urine) and then allowed to rest/grow without being disturbed while other paddocks are grazed.

As a newbie farmer, you will likely need some help with figuring out how much forage your land has on it. Different grass species have varying amounts of nutrition. Consider hiring a consultant who specializes in holistic grazing methods.

Read the following to get your head around the idea of rotational grazing or 'holistically planned grazing'. By managing your land properly, you can maximize the amount of forage for your animals and at the same time substantially increase the productivity of your land. It will require much more effort than simply putting your livestock out to pasture and forgetting about them but it's well worth the effort.

If you want to be inspired by cattle changing deserts into grasslands, watch this Ted Talk by Allan Savory.

Rock Down To Electric Avenue

You may want to serenade your livestock with this tune once you have sectioned off your paddocks using electric fencing...or not. Electric fencing is half the price of traditional barbed wire and unlike traditional wood posts and wire, electric fencing makes it easy to add and remove paddocks at will.

Working with electric fencing is very easy to learn. Yes, you will get shocked a few times but so will your livestock and somehow after you've been shocked you'll feel less guilty when it happens to them. Most livestock are pretty quick at learning to respect the wire. It seems that we humans can take a bit longer to learn.

The most widely used quality electric fencing materials are made by Gallagher. No matter what livestock you're handling or what size of operation you have, they'll have what you need.

It is essential that the outermost fence around your pasture is a traditional barbed wire fence. As great as electric fencing is, it only takes a power outage or a tree falling over the wire and thus shorting the line in order for chaos to ensue. If you know you have a well maintained, 3 or 4 strand barbed wire fence, you will be able to sleep soundly. Inspect your fence line at least once every couple of weeks to sleep even more soundly.

Cattle

There are few sounds associated with farm life as synonymous as the sound of a low moo. There are many 'cow' terms you've likely heard of. Here are the most common and their definitions:

Term	Definition	Extra information
Heifer	A female over 1 year old that has not given birth yet.	
Calf	A male or female that is not yet 1 year old.	
Cow	A female that has given birth.	
Steer	A male that is castrated before	

	it matures sexually.	
Bull	A sexually mature male with all its bits and pieces intact.	Some people refer to all uncastrated males as 'bulls'.
Yearling	A male or female calf older than one year but less than two.	

What Breed of Cattle to Choose

There are a number of factors to consider when choosing a breed. The climate you will be farming in, what you intend to use the animal for (meat vs. milk) and your general preferences will help determine which breed is right for you.

Attend a cattle auction in your area and see what types of cattle are being sold. Not only will you find out which breeds are most likely to do well in your climate, you will also get a very good idea about the price you are likely to pay. An excellent source of information on the most popular meat breeds in North America is below.

You can buy your cows privately or go to your local cattle auction. Befriend a neighbor or someone who knows something about cattle and take them along with you to make sure you don't end up paying more than you need to. It takes an experienced eye to spot potential problems with an animal and costly rookie mistakes are extremely common. If you are simply looking for something to fatten up for meat, choose a steer. That way you won't have to deal with the castration issue. You can also purchase cow/calf pairs and start to breed cattle on your own.

Identifying Large Livestock

Once you've purchased your cattle, it is important to be able to identify them in order to prevent theft or accidental mix-ups. There are several ways in which this is done. Most breeders use at least two of these methods but depending on your herd size; you may be satisfied using just one. Ear tags, freeze brands, paint brands, and electronic ID's are all relatively pain-free ways to identify your animals. Hot brands and tattooing are painful, and you will most likely want to avoid using these methods. A short explanation on each of the methods is here:

Here is a video showing an expert freeze branding. When done properly, this is a very effective method. Unlike the other humane methods listed above, freeze branding can be seen at a distance and this is very helpful if one of your animals breaks free and joins the neighbor's herd.

Breeding

Forget the idea of buying a bull. If you only have a small number of females to impregnate, you are much better off find a vet who can do artificial insemination (AI). A well-bred bull is expensive and even renting one to service your cows or heifers can be very costly. Another benefit of AI is that the vet will do pregnancy testing to make sure that the process was successful. Ask around at the nearest cattle auction house to get the name of an experienced vet. Your vet can recommend what kind of bull semen would work best with your cow breed. Generally speaking if it's a heifer you're dealing with, pick a smaller breed of bull – one that 'throws a small calf'. Heifers can sometimes have more difficulties birthing.

Castration

Oh, what a lovely topic to discuss. So does it hurt the calf/bull/soon to be steer? Yes. And I know you only ask because you are hoping against hope that it doesn't. There are certain aspects of farming that are more than a little off-putting, and this is one of them. Unfortunately, if you are going to have a semi-docile male to deal with before you eat tasty meat, you will need to castrate. Bull meat doesn't have as nice a flavor (although some people disagree) and the personality of bulls can be very aggressive. Remember the 'running of the bulls' that occurs in Spain every year? Yeah. You don't want that.

This fellow has a few interesting things to say about the topic:

/

The following link is a video showing you how to castrate a male. Warning: this may put you off farming completely, flee to the nearest office tower and hide under a desk in a cubicle. On a positive note, you can hire someone to do this for you.

Benefits of Grass-fed Beef

Cows were not meant to eat grain. Like goats and sheep, cattle are ruminants and have a stomach designed to ferment plant-based materials prior to digesting. Cattle are much healthier and in turn their meat is healthier when they are on a 100% plant diet. Omega 3 fatty acids (the kind of Omega's your body wants lots of) are much higher in grass-fed beef versus your grain-fed variety.

Grass-fed beef has a slightly different flavor, but this is how beef is supposed to taste. If you're used to feedlot cattle beef (what you buy in your local grocery store), rest assured that you'll soon get used to the flavor. Grass-fed beef is leaner than grain-fed so to avoid drying it out, make sure to cook it at a lower temperature.

Milk Cows

The 'relationship' you develop with your milk cow will be entirely different than that which you have with other livestock. There's nothing like extracting milk from another animal's teats' to make you grow a little closer. Every day she will be giving you gallons of milk for you to make highly nutritious food when all you do for her is give her a bit of grass and hay. It hardly seems fair and partly because of this you will grow quite fond of her.

When purchasing a milk cow, choose a quality milk breed over one that produces a high quantity of milk. You want to look for cow milk with high butterfat content. The higher the butterfat, the healthier the milk. You also want a milking breed that produces 'A2' milk. Most modern dairy breeds produce 'A1' milk that isn't nearly as good for you. In some countries such as Australia, supermarkets sell 'A2' milk and it is marketed as milk that even lactose intolerant people can enjoy. The only way to be certain if your milk cow is producing 'A2' milk is to have her genetically tested. However, there are two breeds that have high butterfat content and that are most likely producing 'A2' milk; those breeds are Jersey and Guernsey.

Below is a review of the book 'The Devil in the Milk' by Keith Woodford. If you are interested in A1 vs. A2 milk, read his book. If you want the 'Cliff Notes' version, read the review below. The general website WestonAPrice.org is an excellent resource for all raw milk related information. There is also a plethora of information on traditional foods. If you're interested in delving into farming so that you can provide your family with the ideal diet, there is no better resource out there.

Milking Your Cow

Milking a cow is hard work. Back in the day when manual labor was the norm, this was a farm job often delegated to children. Sadly, children pre-1950's were much tougher in a lot of ways than most adults are today. Remind yourself of this when you're milking your cow and then tell yourself to 'suck it up'. After a few weeks, your technique will improve, and it will get much easier. There are large milking machines that you can purchase but unless you have more than 3 or 4 cows to milk, the hassle of sanitizing the machine will be more trouble than it's worth. There are also smaller units that you may want to try if you are having a problem getting the hang of it.

Below is one of the many videos on YouTube you can find of someone milking a cow the old fashioned way.

It is a good idea to get a cow/calf pair when purchasing a milk cow. Firstly, having a calf will mean you will only need to milk once a day instead of twice. Having calf also will enable you to take the odd weekend off if need be without having to worry about begging your neighbor to milk your cow for you. Check out the link below and discover the joys of owning a milk cow. Mastitis

The biggest headache of dealing with a milk cow is if she gets mastitis. Mastitis is the inflammation of the mammary gland and udder. In order to prevent mastitis one of the most important things is to make sure that the cow's udder is properly 'stripped'. The act of stripping a milk cow means that all of the milk is emptied out of the udder and teats. If your cow does end up getting mastitis, there are natural ways to treat the condition. Try to treat her without using antibiotics as this will get into her milk. The link below has information on how to prevent mastitis and treat your animal without drugs. Getting your milk cow completely healthy again will take a lot of time and effort so prevention is key.

Benefits of Raw Milk

The milk you buy from the store is pasteurized and most likely homogenized as well. Pasteurization is heating up milk to a certain temperature in order to kill off bad (and unfortunately good) bacteria that are present. When brucellosis, a disease cattle can get, was common, this precaution made perfect sense. Nowadays this disease is fairly rare due to vaccinations of female cows, and if you go to extra lengths and get your dairy cow tested, you can drink your raw milk with near 100% confidence. Pasteurizing milk essentially 'deadens' it. Instead of ending up with a product rich in gut loving bacteria (in a good way), you end up with a food that isn't nearly as nutritious as what your tough and healthy grandparents had access to.

Homogenization is a mechanical process used to break the fat globules in the milk into smaller sizes that allows for the milk to have a smoother consistency. and some say a longer shelf life. The problem with this is that it turns something au-natural like milk and manufactures it into something else entirely. Some say the smaller fat globules don't jibe well with your body. There is much contradictory information on the internet regarding raw milk. Again, a good resource for information is the Weston A. Price Foundation which is decidedly pro raw milk.

Low Stress Animal Handling

Unfortunately, most livestock operations are still run by people who make a lot of noises to startle the cattle in order to make them move in the direction they want them to go. Do not do this. Leave the "Hi Yah!" for corny old Westerns and become one with nature instead. There is a much better way to handle livestock that keeps your animals calm and still gets them to do what you want them to do. As an added benefit, your livestock will not lose weight when they're being moved around (which stressed cattle do) and they will not say nasty things behind your back.

Bud Williams was a pioneer of low-stress animal handling techniques. His daughter Tina Williams has carried on in her Father's footsteps and teaches at workshops around the world. If you get a chance to attend one of these workshops, it's well worth it. You will view your animals with a new kind of respect and increase your productivity along the way. This article is a little old but as relevant now as it ever was.

Keeping Your Herd Healthy

Minerals & Supplements

One of the hardest parts of being a farmer is being humble enough to realize that Mother Nature probably knows what she's doing. Cattle, being 'smart' in their own particular way, know what they need. That's why allowing them to choose which minerals they want to consume is such a great idea. Most minerals from your local farm supply store come in mixes so if the cattle wants sodium; it has no choice but to also consume magnesium whether or not that is what the cow needs. There is a company called Free Choice Minerals that sells minerals separately along with a special feeder that allows for your cattle to pick and choose what it wants.

Vaccinations

When you purchase your cattle, ask about what vaccinations have been done. Follow up with your local large animal vet and find out which diseases are common in your area. What type of vaccinations your animal will need will depend on a number of risk factors. Keep in mind that one sick animal can soon turn into several sick cattle. Walking out to your pasture and seeing a 1,000 pound dead cow is not a great way to start out your day. There are many ways to cut costs when farming, but delaying or forgoing vaccinating your animals isn't one of the smartest.

Death Comes to Us All

A great line from the movie Braveheart and also something to keep in mind when you're looking down, stunned at your first dead animal. Depressing as it may be, you will have one of your animals die unintentionally. You can do everything right; vaccinate, deter predators, provide ample feed and still you will have an animal die. It pays to be a pragmatist if you're going to be a farmer.

It is a good idea to have an autopsy performed on the animal. Finding out why the animal died can prevent more deaths in your herd. After the autopsy, you will need to decide what to do with the body. The smell of a rotting corpse wafting through the kitchen window isn't too appetizing so deal with it as quickly as possible. If you have access to a backhoe, you can simply dig a hole and bury the animal. If there is a rendering company in your area you can call them and for a fee have them pick up the carcass. Speak to your neighbors or your vet and they can advise what options are the most practical in your area.

This link below lists several dozen diseases and conditions that occur in cattle. I don't suggest looking at it if you're one of those people that gets 'Google happy' looking up possible diseases when you have a headache. There are usually only about a half a dozen possible problems that will occur in your climate and your particular area. Again, talk to your neighbors and your vet and then try not to worry.

When You Want Death to Come

Your options regarding killing your animal are going to depend on the laws in your area. Laws vary State to State and Province to Province. Many of these laws are in place to discourage smaller operations and bolster larger, feedlot operations and slaughter facilities.

If you are farming simply to provide food for your family, probably most if not all of these laws will not apply to your operation. However if you plan on selling some of your meat to your neighbors or at your local farmers market, be very aware of what is legal and what is not.

An ideal scenario is to have a mobile slaughtering service come to your farm. That way the animal won't have the stress of being transported to a strange place and probably spending the night before being killed. Animals are not stupid, and one can assume that if it's not a lush pasture in front of them when the transport doors open, it probably means that their grazing days are through.

A mobile service will kill your animal quickly on site, cut and package your meat and be on their way. It is by far the most humane way to turn your animal into groceries. It doesn't mean you won't still cry but at least you know you've acted in the kindest way a carnivore with a conscience can act. Check out this link and have some tissues ready if you're a softie.

Chickens

When it comes to raising chickens for meat or eggs, you will need to start speaking 'chicken'. Here is a long list of commonly used terms that will have you sounding like an expert to your city friends in no time…whether or not you know what you're doing.

For meat chickens (broilers) and egg chickens (layers), order chicks and have them shipped to you. If there is a local farm supply store, they may have chicks for sale as well. The time of year your chicks are delivered to you is crucial. Temperature is a big factor in whether or not your chicks grow into healthy adults. You will need a warm, safe place to house your chicks before they are old enough to be moved into the portable coop. Brooder boxes and small pens should be purchased and set up before your chicks arrive.

If you order from a large hatchery, you will be able to speak to someone who has shipped chicks to your climate before. They will be able to give you expert advice on what breeds do well in your area and will happily upsell to you all of the chicken rearing products they have available. Resist the urge to splash out a lot of cash. Plan ahead and buy what you absolutely need. You can spend heaps of money on a fancy brooding box or a hundred on a good heat lamp and some plywood.

For U.S. farmers, getting your chicks from McMurray Hatchery is a good bet. They deliver to Canada as well, but you'll need to drive to the border to pick up your chicks.

In the spring, you can often find chicks at your local feed store. Unfortunately, debeaking chicks is very common. De-beaking is when the tip of the chicks' beak is cut off to prevent chickens from pecking one another to death. In large commercial chicken operations, this procedure prevents many deaths. For your farm, it is unnecessary and prevents chickens from properly foraging. Wherever you buy your chicks, make sure to ask whether they have been de-beaked and visually check for any evidence. If you see a bloody red spot on the tip of the beak, don't buy it.

Meat Birds (Broilers)

Broilers are meat birds that have been bred to get large very quickly. They have abnormally big breasts and large legs. Depending on the breed you choose, some are ready to butcher at just eight weeks old. Broilers grow so large and so quickly that by the time they're ready to eat; you may feel like you're putting them out of their misery. If you want more flexibility as to when you want to butcher your birds, pick an older breed. The newer meat bird breeds grow so quickly that if you don't butcher them in time; their oversized bodies can simply drop dead.

Brooding Chicks

Chicks are extremely sensitive to cold. They won't have their mother's feathers to hide under so the temperature in the brooder box should start out at 90-95°F (32-35°C). Every week reduce the temperature in the brooder box or pen by 5 degrees. By week 6, the temperature in the brooder box should closely resemble the outside temperature. Most chicks will have lost the soft down and have adult feathers which will allow them to trap heat close to their bodies.

This website has a lot of great tips on how to care for young chicks.

Chicken Feed

When you first get your chicks, you will need to provide them with a good quality starter feed. Do not give feed that contains antibiotics. When kept in clean and dry conditions, there is no need to medicate chicks. Feeding chicks antibiotics will a have negative effect on the immune system of the bird as well as the quality of eggs and meat that are produced.

You can start feeding chicks pieces of fruit and vegetables almost immediately such as a watermelon rind but make sure to give them access to grit if you decide to do this. You can buy grit for your chicks where you buy feed. Just place grit in a separate food dish and the chicks will help themselves to it as needed. Since chickens don't have teeth to break up larger food particles, grit helps break apart food in their gizzard. Once the chicks have grown up, they are moved into the portable coop, they will get natural grit in the form of small stones and sand from their surroundings.

For your laying hens, grower feed is provided next until the chickens are about 18 weeks old followed by layer feed. Don't make the mistake of switching to layer feed too early.

Meat birds eat a large quantity of food, and if you overfeed them, they can die of heart attacks before its butchering time. There are differing opinions on how often you should feed meat birds but under no circumstances should you have food available to them 24/7.

It's important that the starter feed they're on is about 22-24% protein. They can stay on the same food until they are just about fully grown. For the final couple of weeks, give them feed that has about 16% protein. Feed that is lower in protein is sometimes called finisher feed and will increase the fat content in your birds so you'll end up with a nice, moist roast. If you prefer to have a lower fat content, just continue feeding the high protein feed until butchering time.

The Vegetarian Chicken Myth

One of the most common misconceptions about chickens is that they are vegetarians. You may have noticed egg cartons in the grocery store labeled "Vegetarian Fed" as if it's a good thing. In reality, a vegetarian chicken is about as normal as a carnivorous cow. Chickens are omnivores. Chickens fed a strictly vegetarian diet will lack much-needed nutrients to produce healthy meat and eggs. Using a portable coop will help birds to have access to bugs and other little critters. During winter months when access to grass is limited for laying hens, it is beneficial to supplement grain feed with organ meats.

Avoid feeding your chicken's fish meal. Yes, it boosts Omega 3's in your eggs but it also makes them smell and taste fishy. This can also occur if feed contains crushed shells (used to boost calcium) as many shells will include bits of mussels etc. which are fishy smelling as well. Soy is another form of food to avoid for all of your animals (GM or non-GM). Avoid feeding yourself any kind of soy as well but that's a whole other e-book.

There are many people who advocate feeding chickens eggshells. Nutritionally there are good arguments for doing this as eggshells have high calcium content. That said, be very careful how you do this as it can 'teach' chickens that their own freshly laid egg might be a tasty treat. Make sure the eggshells you feed your chickens are baked and then crushed up. That way their tiny brains won't be able to make the connection between egg shells that were eggs and what they just laid. For both laying hens and meat birds, you will want to provide high quality, non-GM feed. Your local feed store will have what you need, and you can supplement this with kitchen scraps and some raw organ meats.

Below is a good article on feeding chickens the natural way by the good folks at the Weston A. Price Foundation.

Portable Coops

For meat and egg birds, it is best to house them in a cage that is moveable. Access to fresh ground on a daily basis will improve the nutritional quality of your eggs, and your meat will taste better as well. When your chickens have access to pasture including green plants and bugs, they will require less food. You can use your chickens to trim and fertilize your grass while keeping your birds healthy and happy.

Using a portable coop will dramatically lessen the likelihood that your chickens will develop problems with mites. There will also be no smell issue when the chicken coop is moved daily to fresh ground. Foxes love tasty chickens and are eager to take advantage of bottomless cages and dig a hole underneath. Thwart the plans of that clever fox and make sure the floor of your portable coop is made of wire mesh.

You will need at least 4 square feet of space for every chicken you raise. Make sure to have one nesting box for every 4 or 5 chickens. Easy access to the box from the outside of the cage will make your life much easier and disturb your chickens less. Put fresh straw or woodchips in the nesting boxes as needed. There are dozens of websites that show you step by step how to build a portable coop. Remember that it is easier to build a much bigger coop than you need and have too much space than underestimate the size you need and have to deal with overcrowding.

What climate you live in will determine how much weatherproofing you need as well as the design. You will be butchering your meat chickens before winter rolls around, but your laying chickens will need a warm place to spend their winter. Depending on how harsh your winters get, you may need a large enclosed area for these chickens.

The Pecking Order

If you already have a few chickens, you need to be very careful when integrating newer flock members. It is not uncommon for chickens to peck another chicken to death. A rather horrific way to die I imagine. There are a number of things that can be done to prevent this conflict from ever happening. The easiest thing to do is to make a small wire mesh cage and place it beside your portable coop. These 'play pens' allow your established chickens to see and hear your new arrivals.

After a week, you can allow the little ones into the larger enclosure. But keep a close eye on the dynamics that unfold. It is natural for a 'pecking order' to be enforced or adjusted, but excessive bullying to the point of bloodshed must be stopped immediately.

Remove the bullied chicken back to the playpen for a few days and allow it to heal fully, and then re-introduce her. If the bullying continues, give the perpetrator a time-out in the playpen for a few days. Nine times out of ten, she will adjust her attitude. One time out of ten, you will have a lovely roast chicken.

When you transfer the new chickens into the portable coop, keep the nesting boxes closed for a few days. Nesting boxes make a great place for youngsters to hide and feel safe in, but they also will poop while they hide. Poop plus eggs = nasty bacteria in your omelet. Your established laying hens can tough it out for a few days and lay eggs on the ground. They may be grouchy about it, but they'll deal. Once they have gotten over their shyness and learned to sleep up on the roost, open your nesting boxes again, and all should be fine.

Cow and Chicken Harmony

One of the best ways to prevent an abundance of flies on your farm is to move your portable coop behind your cattle. The chickens will love pecking about in the cow patties and eating the fly larva. They will also help to spread the cow patty around which will help fertilize a larger area of soil. It's one of those win-win solutions brought to you by good old Mother Nature. Make sure that your cattle are in a separate pasture before moving in the chicken coop as the frame of the chicken coop can make for a tempting scratching post.

The Rooster: Just a Pretty Face

Unless you want to hatch eggs, there is no need for you to own a rooster. When you purchase chicks, they are sexed; in other words it is unlikely you will receive a male unless you want one. The biggest disadvantage to having a rooster around when you have laying hens is that you end up with fertilized eggs (a red spot in the yolk). Some don't mind these eggs – there is nothing 'wrong' with eating one. However, it is unappetizing to many people.

Chicken Health

Lice and Mites

One of the most common health issues with chickens are mites and lice. A portable coop will greatly reduce the likelihood that you'll have to deal with this. Evidence of mites are found on eggs in the form of tiny red spots. If you part the feathers on your chickens and look closely, you will see the little creepy crawlies easily. Lice eggs can often visible at the base of the feathers.

The following link has pictures of what to look for and tips on prevention and treatment. Try not to start scratching.

This video shows step by step how to rid your chickens of mites and prevent re-infection.

And lastly, a very detailed description on how to get rid of chicken lice…not to be confused with chicken fried rice.

Molting

In the fall when the days start getting shorter, chickens will start to lose their feathers. It can take many weeks for them to re-grow new ones and during this time they will need extra protein in their diets. Consider adding extra organ meats to their regular food.

During this time, your hens will either lay less often or quit laying eggs altogether. In fact all through the winter, egg production will fall dramatically to the point where many of your hens will only produce an egg every three days or so. Once spring and summer roll around, egg production will increase again.

Butchering Chickens

Why Did the Chicken Cross the Road? Not because it wanted to die, that's for sure. Unfortunately for meat birds, that is their lot in life. Emotionally speaking, it is easier for most people to deal with killing a chicken when compared with killing a steer. Below is a step by step guide on how to kill, pluck and butcher your chickens.

If you haven't ever killed a chicken, try to find a local farm that has free-range chickens and volunteer to help them kill and butcher. Killing one chicken after another will soon get you used to the idea. Working with a big group of people who view the process as no big deal will help get your head around the idea. What was once a chicken will begin to simply look like meat. And that my friend is how you evolve from a city slicker into a real farmer.

Here is Joel Salatin of Polyface Farms to walk you through the process.

Grocery Store Con

The best thing about raising meat birds is how much better tasting they are than what you find in a grocery store. Supermarket birds are pumped full of antibiotics and added water (you're paying based on weight). This meat is bland tasting and potentially harmful. The harmful bacteria that are present at many processing plants where the animals are killed and butchered just add to the health concerns. There is no doubt that the way in which most chickens are raised is a danger to our health.

A chicken with lots of room to roam will be unlikely ever to get sick and has no need of antibiotics. The meat will be flavorful and nutrient dense. Chickens that forage will have meat with higher levels of Omega 3 fatty acids and Vitamin E. Lastly, you will be eating a chicken that once had a happy life thanks to you. So enjoy your drumstick without the guilt.

Turkeys

Young turkeys are pullets and should be brooded separately from your chicks. The temperature needed in the brooding box is exactly the same as with chicks but they require a different type of feed. Turkeys need to be fed game bird feed that has about 28% protein. After they are about 12 weeks old, they can start to eat feed with about 22-24% protein. Like chickens, you can use a finisher feed for the last few weeks to increase fat content.

Once moved from the brooder box or pen, you can raise turkeys alongside chickens without any problems. Just make sure that your portable coop has enough room as a full grown turkey is significantly bigger than a chicken and things can get a bit crowded. Turkeys are butchered at about 22 weeks old. So mark Thanksgiving on your calendar, count backward and put in your order for pullets.

Here is a long, step by step video on how to butcher a turkey.

Duck…Duck…Goose!

Waterfowl are much hardier than both chickens and turkeys. They are less susceptible to disease and don't need to be kept in a brooder box as long because they grow more rapidly and get their feathers earlier. They also need a bit lower temperature when in the brooder box/pen. For goslings and ducklings, start at about 90°F and reduce by 5-10° per week until 70° is reached. At that point, the little ones can be released into a portable coop. Both goslings and ducklings should be started on a 50-50% mixture of poultry starter and game bird starter. Make sure that your feed is un-medicated as ducklings can become very sick if fed antibiotics.

Young goslings can subsist almost entirely on grass while ducklings cannot forage as well so will need to be fed throughout their lives. Geese are voracious eaters and can mow down grass very efficiently. It is a good idea to keep ducks and geese separate from chickens and turkeys for this reason.

If you have a small number of geese, consider letting them roam freely on your farm. They are easy to herd and have a strong homing instinct so it is unlikely that they will be lost. Since they need little to no supplemental feed, they are very self-sufficient. Just make sure there is water available for them to drink. If you are planning on raising more than a half a dozen geese, do put them in a confined, portable cage. Although you may not think you geese are as capable of overgrazing as you larger livestock, they can and will. For the most part, you should incorporate all of your livestock into your rotational grazing plan.

The Patient Butcher

Depending on the breed of duck, you can butcher as early as 7 weeks while geese can be killed as early as 9 weeks. Compared with chickens and turkeys, butchering a duck is very time consuming because the feathers are difficult to remove. Ducks and geese also have a layer of gossamer down under their regular feathers which keep them waterproof. Removing gossamer requires the patience of a Zen master so take deep breaths.

It is easier to pluck a duck or goose if you butcher at specific times. For ducks, the easiest butchering times are at 7, 12.5, or 18 weeks old. If you choose to butcher in between these specific time periods for geese or ducks, you will need more than the patience of a Zen master to get through it. Trying to pluck out the feathers will drive you mad. Below is a step by step guide on butchering a duck.

For geese, you can butcher at 9, 15, or 20 weeks old. Geese are very intelligent, and it can be heart wrenching to catch one. Below is a non-gruesome video just on the catching of a goose. A large sack and something to bind the legs together helps immensely.

Pigs

Pigs are perhaps the most underrated livestock when considering how much meat can be produced in a given time frame with one pregnant female. Pigs are intelligent, full of personality, and relatively easy to take care of. Plus without pigs there would not be bacon. Nuff said.

Here are some basic terms to become familiar with if you're considering raising pigs.

Land Needed

For happy, healthy pigs it's best to mimic the type of habitat where wild pigs reside as closely as possible. Wild pigs live in wooded areas with access to water. They are clean, organized animals that like separate places to rest, cool down, roll around, and defecate. It is important to remember that pigs have no sweat glands except for one its' snout. For that reason you must provide a mud hole or some other means in order to keep your pig cool during hot days.

Pig Breeds

You will want to search out a heritage breed that does well in your climate. Pigs that are raised in commercial settings have long since lost any natural 'forage' instincts that their ancestors had and will not be able to function in a free-range environment. Here are some of the most common heritage pig breeds found in North America. A favorite of these and one of the most widely available is the Tamworth.

The "Pigness of the Pig"

Joel Salatin is known for saying that we must "respect the pigness of the pig". In order for pigs to be raised in a healthy way, we need to understand what they're needs and habits are and provide an environment that suits them. Below is one of the many videos you can find online with Joel and his pigs. Dr. Mercola, who he is speaking with, is a vocal proponent of free-range animals and traditional eating.

Pigs are very social animals and live in stable family groups. The basic 'pig family' would consist of between one and four sows along with their offspring. Boars keep apart and to themselves generally. During mating season, they join the females. It is unwise to disturb this natural social order and separate animals that are used to being together.

Paddock Pigs and Avoiding Escapes

Like all livestock, it's best to move pigs from paddock to paddock. You will need to set up a rotational grazing system using the same 'animal unit' principles that were discussed earlier. Electric fencing will need to be lower to the ground and should be three strands. Be sure to have one strand close enough to the ground to deter piglets from escaping.

Even though you are smarter than a pig, a pig has dedicated much time and energy into thinking of ways to escape. It's possible he's even thought ahead of routes he can take to avoid being caught once he has escaped. Catching a pig that doesn't want to be caught is very difficult (although hilarious to watch from an outsider's perspective). In order not to be driven mad by pigs, keep them happy. If humane treatment isn't enough motivation, think of your sanity.

Rooting Around

Pigs will eat almost anything…so watch your back. In all seriousness though, it may surprise you that they will eagerly seek out rodents and frogs along with rooting around for tubers, nuts, and berries. They graze grass and other vegetation as well. You can buy a dry mix feed at your local farm feed store and mix it according to the directions. Toss in any kitchen scraps and rotate your pigs regularly to fresh pasture, and you should have happy pigs.

Adorable Piglets

A mature female usually has two litters of piglets a year. Each litter can contain anywhere between 5 and 10 piglets. Even before you do the math, you can see how productive this animal is. The gestation period of a sow is 115 days and a few days before she gives birth she will separate herself from her family unit and make a 'nest'. If you're curious about whether or not she's given birth, spy on her from afar. Pigs do not normally have any trouble giving birth and like all animals, she would prefer to do so in private.

After giving birth, she will mostly lie on her side for the first few days and encourage her piglets to nurse. Within a few days she will have active piglets that will follow her wherever she goes and squeal when they want a suck.

It is best to let mother and piglets bond and intervene as little as possible. Once the piglets are a week old and becoming more independent, the sow will be very protective. Stay away during this period and wait until the sow and piglets have re-joined the family group before you attempt to interact with the piglets. Always gauge how the show feels about your presence before getting too involved. After about 3 weeks, piglets will start to eat some solid foods and will naturally wean themselves between 13-17 weeks old.

Pig House

During winter months, pigs will need a warm, dry place to rest. There are many inexpensive design ideas you can find on the internet. What you will need to construct will depend on how chilly your winters are and how many pigs you plan on housing. A low built, three sided structure is ideal. The roof need be only about four feet high. Provide ample amounts of straw and or leaves for bedding.

The Little Piggy Went to Market

There are few sounds as horrific as a 'stuck pig'. Unlike killing a chicken, killing a pig will likely be fairly difficult. Firstly a pig is a much smarter animal so you will likely find it takes a greater emotional toll on you. Secondly, pigs are substantially bigger and butchering a large animal for beginners is difficult.

For first timers, it is best to call a mobile butchery. Perhaps if you have and steer and a porker ready at the same time, you can fill two freezers at once. If you have a real desire to jump into the deep end after raising your first porker, follow these steps and Godspeed.

You can taste the happiness in free-range pork. Pork from commercial operations lacks the flavor and depth that pastured pork has. And like other commercially raised meat, it is also lacking in Omega 3's.

These websites explain the science behind why pastured pork and other free-range animal products are best. Once you've tasted what your grandparents used to eat and are aware of how animals are treated in commercial factory farms, it's hard to go back to buying meat at the grocery store.

Sheep & Goats

A glossary of commonly used sheep and goat terms can be found here:

The topics of sheep and goats are being covered at the same time because they share many of the same characteristics. Wool sheep are impractical to raise unless you are very experienced and have a large number of animals.

Best Meat Breeds

The most popular meat sheep breed in North Amei.
Dorper. This breed is originally from South Africa and i.
extremely hardy and adaptable. There is no need to sheer a
Dorper because their coat is a combination of wool and
hair that simply drops off. Dorpers grow quickly and
produce a great tasting meat.

For goats, you can't go wrong with Boars. Like Dorpers,
Boars are also a South African breed. They are also hardy
and adaptable but a little more so than sheep. Goats are
much smarter than sheep and less likely to drop dead for
seemingly no reason. The popularity of these breeds means
that you will likely be able to find an adequate number of
animals to start your flock/herd.

Rams & Bucks

You will need approximately one ram and one buck for
every 5-10 ewes or does. However, this ratio depends on
whether the female stock is 'in season' or not. The process

of your mature females falling pregnant requires careful planning and observation.

Twins

One of the benefits of sheep and goats is that you can multiply your flock/herd much more quickly than you can with cattle. Twins can be very common with both sheep and goats, but it will take some time, organization and a bit of luck to make this a reality on your farm. The genes of both males and females play a part. It is important to keep track of which animal gave birth to twins and identify those twins so that when the females come into maturity, they are kept and bred as well. Getting your flock/herd to produce the maximum amount of offspring (while keeping their health a top priority) should be your goal.

Avoiding Birthing Issues

In the case of sheep, birth issues can be common. Mostly this depends on the breed of sheep you are raising. If your breed is native to Western Europe, you may encounter more problems. The reason for this is because many farmers in this region of the world would 'help' ewes birth their lambs when they had difficulties. Ewes with problems birthing produced female offspring that inherited this bad trait and after many generations, it became the norm that a farmer needed to 'help' during lambing season.

In other parts of the world, land holdings are so vast that when ewes give birth there is no human around to help. Ewes that are unable to birth without intervention died along with their lamb and were consumed by the nearest wolf or some such predator. A tragic end indeed unless you look at it from a Darwinian standpoint. When considering how to manage your flock (or other livestock for that matter), think long term. Obviously it would be a bad idea to let mother and offspring die. That said, if you want to avoid sleepless nights and heartache in the long term, prevention is key. If for any reason, your female livestock have trouble birthing, make sure to cull her and eventually cull her offspring. In properly bred livestock, birthing should happen easily.

Castration

To prevent aggressiveness towards other sheep and goats, young males should be castrated at approximately seven weeks. Also, uncastrated male goats and sheep stink. It's fine if you have only a few bucks and rams to service your females running around but the stench is pretty horrible if half of your herd smells that bad. So do your nose a favor and call in your vet.

Rotational Grazing and Shelter

Sheep and goats can be grazed alongside cattle, so there is no need to have separate paddocks. Goats are browsers preferring to eat plant matter that cattle and sheep don't particularly like. Goats are also much more intelligent than sheep or cattle so you will need to make certain your fencing is adequate. A four strand electric fence should suffice.

Sheep and goats are much less hardy than cattle. Both will require shelter when the weather gets rough. A low, three sided shelter with some straw bedding will work fine. It is important, especially in the case of goats, that they keep dry.

Goat Milk

For many farmers, having a milk goat makes a lot more sense than having a milk cow. For one, goats are easier to handle due to their small size. Exactly how much milk a goat produces will depend on the breed, how often you are milking and whether or not she is nursing a kid.

All goat milk is A2 milk (the kind you want) and like cow milk, the higher the butterfat content, the more nutritious it will be. That said, what type of products you plan on making with your milk is a factor in deciding how much butterfat will be most useful to you. Goat milk is very versatile; you can make cheese as well as soap and lotion.

Decide on what products you're most keen on producing and then research which breed is right for your family.

Like cow's, goat's teats and udders require similar care. The link below shows the benefits of a goat milking contraption.

Soap

Goat milk soap helps a variety of skin conditions such as dry skin, eczema, and psoriasis. It also contains natural nutrients that you will not find in store bought soap including alpha hydroxyl acids, Vitamin A, and selenium. The fat that goat's' milk contains also has a great moisturizing effect. Below is a step by step guide on how to make soap.

Say Cheese

Making cheese is something you either love or hate. Precise measurements and close attention must be paid in order to be successful. Goat milk produces excellent tasting cheese. Just make sure you stay in the kitchen and always keep your eye on the thermometer. Making cheese and multitasking do not mix well.

Milking Sheep

Some people say that sheep milk is the healthiest milk, and many prefer the taste of sheep milk over both cow and goat milk. The only drawback to milking a sheep versus a goat is that sheep are skittish creatures and have a little bit of a problem relaxing enough to be milked. So even though you can milk a sheep, it's a bit more difficult which is probably why we don't see a lot of 'sheep milk soap' for sale.

Here is a fun and informative comparison of the three most common types of milk.

Sheep & Goat Health

Foot Rot

Foot rot is a common problem in sheep and goats, and wet conditions exacerbate the problem. The bacteria can take hold if proper measures to prevent the disease are not in place and can spread rapidly within your flock/herd. Rotational grazing is one preventative tool that can keep your animals free from this painful condition. Since moist conditions make matters worse, always have a dry spot available for your animals to find shelter and change bedding frequently.

Check your animals twice yearly and trim hooves yearly or more often if needed. If one of your animals is limping, separate it from the other animals and find out if foot rot is the issue. If so, keep the sheep or goat separated until it is fully recovered. In some cases, foot rot is very difficult to get rid of so it may be easier to cull the animal.

The following paper examines various preventative measures and treatments. Keep in mind that many farmers are not using rotational grazing. You may never have to deal with foot rot at all.

Needed/Deadly Copper

Goats need copper in their diet whereas a build-up of copper in sheep can kill them. In order to avoid this scenario playing out, feed your goats a copper supplement separately from the sheep.

Mary's Tasty Little Lamb

Again I recommend paying a mobile butcher to travel to your farm and process your animals. But if you're eager to do it yourself, check out this website. Included is how to do a halal killing. With a halal killing, the animal bleeds to death. The larger the animal is, the slower the death. Unless you have an absolute need to kill your animal in this fashion, do the humane thing and kill your animal as quickly and painlessly as possible.

Pastured lamb and chevon (goat meat) are highly nutritious. They contain high amounts of those good ol' Omega 3's. If you've never tasted goat meat, you're in for a treat. Goat meat has a slightly milder flavor than lamb so if you like lamb, you'll be pleased with chevon as well.

Bees

Bees are one of the most interesting things you can farm. Whereas we interact with livestock, bees seem to exist in an entirely different world. They go about their day, pollinating plants and producing an amazing product all while ignoring our existence.

Beekeeping is as close to an art form as any type of farming. Nobody knows how long man has been practicing beekeeping, but there is much evidence that the Ancient Egyptians did so and there was even honey discovered in a tomb. The honey was still edible. Honey is the only food that does not spoil.

The Sting

Before deciding on whether to get honey bees, try and jog your memory and think back to whether you've ever been stung by a bee. If you've had any negative reaction to bee stings in the past, it might be a good idea to leave the bee keeping to someone else. Unfortunately, allergic reactions from bee stings often get progressively worse. If you've had bad swelling or anaphylactic reaction in the past, you could be risking your life.

And yes, you will get stung. Probably on average a half dozen times a year even if you're careful and even if you wear protective gear. When you get stung, do not attempt to pull out the stinger. At the end of each stinger, there is venom sack. When you pull out the stinger, you are squeezing the venom into your skin. Instead, find something thin and hard (a card from your wallet would work) and scrape off the stinger. If you're lucky, you won't even end up with a red mark.

Food Variety

Nowadays it is popular to have city bees. At face value, it might seem impractical to have been in the city. After all, how could bees possibly survive let alone thrive in a city versus the country? The answer lies in the diversity in city vegetation versus the monoculture that exists on most farms.

Bees travel about 3-5 miles from their hive. In the city, there are hundreds of gardens and parks within this two mile radius. And each small space offers the bees different varieties of plants that flower at different times of the year. In contrast, much of the countryside has large ¼ section blocks of land with only one type of plant being grown on it. So for a week or two of every year there is a plethora of alfalfa nectar and then that food source disappears, and there may be next to nothing for the bees to eat.

It is important that before you get bees that you take a look around you and ask yourself whether you would want to live there if you were a bee. Bee honest with yourself (I will limit myself to that one bee pun for the remainder of this section).

The Hive

Before purchasing bees, you will need to purchase or build yourself a hive. One of the easiest hive designs to work with is called a Warre Hive. This hive design has been widely used since the early 20th century. One of the best things about the design is that the beekeeper need only open the hive once a year to harvest the honey. The less frequently your bees are disturbed, the better.

http://warre.biobees.com/

Since Warre hives are very popular, you can probably find one to purchase in your area. But if you're keen on a DIY project, click the link below for a video on how it's done.

Here is an excellent and classic resource for all things beekeeping. The author is the inventor of the Warre hive.

Bee Races

Different bee types are categorized as 'races'. You have your Caucasians and your Russians and Italians. Popular races in North America are listed here:

You may have heard about Colony Collapse Disorder (CCD) that has been affecting an increasing number of hives around the world. It is worrisome to many people we need bees to pollinate many of the foods we eat. Without bees, much of our food sources would cease to exist.

As with all diseases, the healthy should be separated from the sick. In the U.S.A., the vast majority of hives are shipped to California for the almond season. These conditions allow for bee diseases to spread rapidly. Bees from these same hives are sold to beginner beekeepers that unbeknownst to them are starting out with diseased bees. Ask questions about where your bees have traveled and where there has been a history of CCD in the area before investing your time and money. Bees can be shipped to you from around the world so if you're having problems sourcing bees locally, look for bees overseas.

Bee Family

A hive consists of one queen bee. It is the queen bee's job to lay enough eggs to make sure the population of the hive is being maintained or increased. The queen can live between 2 and 5 years. When she is nearing the end of her life, the worker bees feed a special diet of 'royal jelly' to about a dozen larvae. This diet allows the larvae to develop into a sexually mature female – a queen bee. The first one to fully form into a queen bee will seek out her 'sisters' and kill them.

The worker bees make up the majority of the bees in the hive and are all female. When they are young, they nurse the larva. As they get older they become scout bees and gather pollen, and they produce the honeycomb. Worker bees work themselves to death – they only live about a month. In the cold, dormant season, they live much longer.

Drones are male, and their only job is to mate with the queen; more often than not it is a queen from a different hive. They do not collect pollen or tend to baby bees. When winter comes around, they are often kicked out of the hive due to scarce resources. Since drones do not protect the hive, they do not have a stinger. They are docile and only leave the hive if the weather is nice. Only a few of the drones ever get a chance to mate. Nature can be cruel though as those that do mate die immediately afterward due to having a barbed sex organ.

Populating Your Hive

You will want your bees to arrive at the end of spring or beginning of summer when nectar from flowers has started to flow. The video below shows you how to move your bees into a beehive.

Nectar, Pollen & Honey

Bees collect nectar and pollen. They have a long tongue like thing to suck up the nectar that they digest and then 'throw up' honey. They use this honey as an energy source, and we humans harvest it. Pollen is collected by the bees as well. They have little hairs all over their bodies that the pollen sticks to. Bees use this pollen as a source of protein and combine it with nectar to make 'bee bread' which they feed to baby bees. If you want to see a video explaining nectar and pollen in the most simplistic way possible, click on the video link below.

Collecting Honey

In the autumn, honey is collected. One beehive can make between 50-200 pounds of honey a year. A smoker is used so that the bees leave the upper frames and settle in the lower frames. Then one by one the upper frames of the hive are removed and placed in an 'extractor'. The extractor spins the frames so that the honey separates from the comb. The website below has practical tips for beekeeping beginners on how to make honey harvest day run as smoothly as possible.

Winterizing the Hive

Even though they are small in size, honey bees are raised all over the world and when their hives are properly 'winterized', they can live through the harshest winters. Properly winterizing your hive can be time-consuming. In order to make sure there is enough food for all of the workers, you will need to kill many of the drones.

Bees don't hibernate. They form a cluster ball with the queen in the middle. The bees nearest the inside keep warm and the ones on the outside vibrate their wings to generate heat. They take turns being on the outside and inside except for the queen. It is important that you leave enough honey after your harvest for the bees to consume during the winter. That will be their only source of food until the weather warms up and they are once again able to collect nectar and pollen. If you accidentally haven't left them enough honey, give them sugar water to eat.

Bee hives can get mite infestations during the winter. To prevent that, make grease patties using the following ingredients:

4.4 pounds (2 kg) granulated sugar

3 ounces (90 ml) corn oil

1.5 pounds (0.7 kg) vegetable shortening (Crisco)

1 pound (454 g) honey

1/2 pound (227 g) mineral salt (pink color)

2.2 ounces (65 ml) wintergreen oil (or tea tree oil)

Use protective gloves and mix the ingredients well with your hands. Make sure the salt is evenly mixed throughout. Make patties about the size of a small hamburger and separate each patty with wax paper. Store in the freezer in plastic bag until you're ready to use them. Place two patties per hive on the top of the frames.

The bees don't like this concoction and will break up the patties and spread them around the hive which is exactly what you want to happen because the patties prevent the spread of mites. The link below contains a plethora of information on how to winterize your hives.

Benefits of Consuming and Using Honey

When consumed, honey has been shown to help reduce the frequency of coughs and alleviate acid reflux. Many people who suffer from hay fever use locally produced honey to ward off the effects of seasonal allergies. Ayurvedic practitioners have been using honey for a variety of conditions for over 4,000 years. It has been claimed that honey improves eyesight, aids in weight loss, and helps combat diarrhea and nausea.

Even though honey contains sugar, the body reacts to it much differently than processed white sugar. Because honey has a specific balance of fructose and glucose, consuming honey can regulate blood sugar levels.

Honey has antibacterial and antifungal properties, and when it is applied externally to burns and wounds, healing can occur more quickly. The wound should first be cleaned and dried before a thin layer of honey is applied. Dress the wound and make sure there isn't any sticky honey leaking out. The dressing should be changed every 24 hours.

Try Before You Buy

Before buying land and animals, it's a good idea to gain some hands-on knowledge. The only way to do that is to 'live' the farming lifestyle. An affordable way to do this is WWOOF'ing. Willing Workers On Organic Farms is a non-profit organization that hooks up farms looking for cheap (i.e. free) labor and those wanting to learn about farming using organic methods.

Whether or not you want to farm using organic methods, volunteering to work on a farm is probably the best idea to save yourself from making costly mistakes. Find a farm that is producing products that you want to produce also. There is nothing you will be able to learn from any book that can compare with doing. It's possible that after a stay at a farm that you will decide that raising pigs isn't what you want to do and instead you're more interested in goats.

When staying at a host farm, be prepared to work hard. Given that there are many ways of farming even one commodity, it's ideal if you can visit a few farms. Be sure to choose farms that are in a similar climate to the one you are considering settling in. Raising chickens in Texas is a whole lot different to raising them in Manitoba. There is no better investment of time you can make than working on a farm before buying one of your own.

The following links will provide information on how to volunteer on a farm near you.

A Farmer's Footprint

They say the best fertilizer is a farmer's footprints'. In other words, in order for your farm to be successful, you need to be physically on the land. There will be no boss telling you what to do next and no deadlines to get work completed so you will need to be self-motivated. If it's a nice, sunny day outside, get working. Having rain for a week straight can throw a monkey wrench into your plans. There are plenty of lazy farmers out there and plenty of bankrupt ones too. So get to work.

JAN - - 2022

SZNCWI
JUL - - 2022

Manufactured by Amazon.ca
Bolton, ON

21378469R00052